THE NPM SIX SESSION LESSON PLAN
A parish program for Basic Liturgical Education

Virgil C. Funk

For
MUSIC IN CATHOLIC WORSHIP
The Bishop's Committee on the Liturgy

With
THE NPM COMMENTARY
as A Teacher's Manual

The Pastoral Press
National Association of Pastoral Musicians
Washington, DC

ISBN: 0-912405-60-0
c 1988 by The Pastoral Press

The Pastoral Press
225 Sheridan Street, NW
Washington, DC 20011
(202) 723-1254

The Pastoral Press is the publications division of the National Association of Pastoral Musicians, a membership organization of musicians and clergy dedicated to fostering the art of musical liturgy.

Printed in the United States of America

CONTENTS

Introduction	3
SESSION ONE The Theology of Celebration	6
SESSION TWO Pastoral Planning for Celebration	9
SESSION THREE The Place of Music in the Celebration	11
SESSION FOUR The Role of Music in the Entrance Rite and the Liturgy of the Word	13
SESSION FIVE The Liturgy of the Eucharist	16
SESSION SIX The Sacraments of Baptism, Anointing of the Sick, Reconciliation, Confirmation and Marriage, and the Burial Rites	19
Bibliography	21

Introduction

This is lesson plan for a course of six session on Catholic Worship.

THE PRESUMPTIONS

About the setting - that this course is being presented to a parish, most likely a parish liturgy committee, composed of people who have little technical knowledge of the liturgy.

About the teacher - that the course is being presented by a person who is leader or a teacher, but not necessarily professionally trained in liturgy. Perhaps the person is the chairperson of the parish liturgy committee, appointed by the pastor.

About the students - that the students are not going to do extensive reading for the course, but are interested in doing some minimum amount of preparation.

About the course length - that the course will last for six sessions, with a minimum of one hour per session.

About the course goal - to prepare the liturgy committee to assume more competently the leadership in preparing liturgical celebrations in the parish.

About the textbook - that *Music in Catholic Worship*, the document published by the Bishop's Committee on the Liturgy in 1972, revised in 1982, (USCC Publication) is the textbook for the class.

About the teacher's manual - that *Music in Catholic Worship, NPM Commentary*, Virgil C. Funk, ed, (The Pastoral Press, 1981) serves as the teacher's manual.

THE TEACHING METHOD

With these presumptions, this **Six Session Lesson Plan** that you are reading now is designed to turn *Music in Catholic Worship: NPM Commentary* into a teacher's manual and *Music in Catholic Worship (MCW)* as the student's textbook.

For each lesson, the teacher should (1) read the appropriate section of *Music in Catholic Worship*, (2) then study the lesson plan given here, especially noting "the points" to be made in that session. (3) If one or several of the points are not understood by the teacher, the teacher should then turn to the teacher's manual, *Music in Catholic Worship: NPM Commentary* and read the appropriate section for more information. At this point, a good teacher will develop his/her own version of these lesson plans. (4) At the end of each class, assign the appropriate section in *Music in Catholic Worship* for the next session.

These six lessons follow the outline contained in *Music in Catholic Worship*, and utilizes the scholarship and comments of the various authors in *Music in Catholic Worship:NPM* as resource for the teacher.

The best material in the hands of the committed teacher presented to interested students is the ideal teaching and learning situation. An option might be that the teaching role might rotate from week to week among the committee members on the principle that teaching is often the best form of learning. Good teachers will know how to adapt this material for their own use.

THE PREPARATION FOR THE PROGRAM

Establish the dates three months (and six, if possible) in advance. Obtain appropriate approval, endorsement, support from the parish staff. Reserve the facility.

Our suggestion is to hold classes six consecutive weeks in a row. Others may do it over months, e.g as the first part of the regular liturgy committee meeting; one hour for education, one hour for general meeting.

The students should be able to sign up for it.

They must get a copy of *Music in Catholic Worship* for a text book. The teacher should have at least four lesson plans completed before the first class begins.

ADVERTIZING AND PROMOTING THE PROGRAM

If the program is for the liturgy committee, it should be promoted directly to that group. This program may also be given to all parishioners. When it is, this is especially successful if the parish liturgy committee has completed the program first, then the outline of the six classes should be announced to the parish in parish bulletins, flyers, promotional material containing: title, date, place, time, length, teacher(s), purpose, and who it is for, what they will learn.

SESSION ONE
The Theology of Celebration

Music in Catholic Worship #1-9
Music in Catholic Worship: NPM Commentary, pp. 3-29.

TEACHER'S PREPARATION:(Suggested approach)
　　Read #1-9 in *Music in Catholic Worship*. Then read the lesson plan below. Take a separate sheet and make your own plan for the class, dividing the class into brief (5-10 minute) segments. If needed, refer to the appropriate section of the teacher's manual *Music in Catholic Worship: NPM Commentary*.
　　This first lesson plan calls for eight sections (viz.,an introduction, five points to make while teaching, and a discussion period followed by assignment for next class). With this in mind, read point one below, and then read Kavanagh's chapter (pp. 5-8) seeking ideas on how to get across the point: "that liturgy means to DO the action". Repeat this procedure for points (3,4,5,6)

GOALS:
To teach these five points:
* That liturgy means to do the action.
* That liturgical celebration presupposes an existing faith community.
* That worship is supposed to have feeling, and that music is critical for affective worship.
* That "good celebrations foster and nourish faith. poor celebrations weaken or destroy faith".
* That Signs are all important to liturgy.

CLASS OUTLINE:
Introduction

　　a. We must learn terms connected with the study of the liturgy, but we need to avoid jargon, meaningless phrases. Liturgy has meaning in human terms and that is what we study.
　　b. Explain how the textbook is *Music in Catholic Worship*, a document published by the Bishop's Com-

mittee on the Liturgy in 1972 (re-published in 1982). Stress it is an American Document. (Give out text) Read aloud sections 1-9.

First Point:
That liturgy means to do the action.
   a. As the teacher, you will stress that Liturgy is something to be done, not watched. It requires words, but also gesture, actions, and most of all, meaning.
   b. For further information on this section, re-read Kavanagh, pp. 5-8.

Second Point:
That liturgical celebration presupposes an existing Faith Community.
   a. If you don't have a faith community, liturgy is not likely to happen. Not every failure should be blamed on the liturgy.
   b. Re-read Norris, pp. 9-13.

Third Point:
The role of feeling and the role of music in liturgy.
   a. Liturgy is the work of the people, a human act. It deals with birthing, eating, washing, marriage, mourning, and leadership, in relationship to God. Stress the human foundations of the liturgy.
   b. Re-read Melloh, pp. 15-20.

Fourth Point:
That "Good celebrations foster and nourish faith. Poor Celebrations weaken and destroy faith."
   a. We are as good a lover as we are sign-maker. When we fail to make good signs, we fail to communicate our love. For those who lead and plan liturgies, the liturgy requires first understanding the purpose and function of the signs and then the reverent care for the signs.
   b. Re-read Walsh, pp. 23-26.

Summary
That Signs are all important to liturgy.
   a. Get the group to think about how signs work,

what is the nature of signs, and how signs work in the liturgy.
    b. Re-read Krosnicki, pp. 27-29 and Kavanagh # 5-8

Suggested Activity: Group discussion on Signs

NEXT CLASS:
    Topic: "Pastoral Planning for Celebration"
    Assignment: Read *Music in Catholic Worship* # 10-12 (Option: Re-Read # 1-9)

SESSION TWO
Pastoral Planning for Celebration

Music in Catholic Worship #10-22.
Music in Catholic Worship: NPM Commentary, pp. 33-58

TEACHERS PREPARATION:
The procedure is the same as the last class. You would benefit from reading Austin Fleming's, *Preparing for Liturgy*, The Pastoral Press.

GOALS:
Teach these four points:
* That you must spend time in preparing liturgy
* That the differences of parishes and parish assemblies is central to planning
* That you begin preparing major feasts and seasons
* That the presider/celebrant must be present

CLASS OUTLINE:
First Point
REVIEW last class: the Importance of Signs.
Distinguish between planning and preparing. The liturgy is a given, we do not reinvent the liturgy for each celebration. Therefore, we do not plan in the sense of re-creating the liturgy from scratch. We prepare the liturgy, with care and reverence so that the signs our clear and effective.

Second Point
That you must spend time in preparing the liturgy.
a. This is a "thank you" for spending the time in this session, and an appeal for those attending this session, to take the time to prepare the liturgies for the parish they serve. Preparation includes ministers, music, readings, space, visual, and above all, personal.
b. In dealing with unity in the liturgy, the metaphor of the many sided diamond refracting the light from many sources is more accurate than a lesson plan where the first reading follows the second reading, as point after point. Liturgy is not a classroom.

c. Planning is something other than preparing lists. (re-read Fleming: Preparing for Liturgy)

Third Point
That the differences of parishes and parish assemblies is central to planning.
 a. What is the diversity of our parish? What are the characteristics of our parish. List them.
 b. Reread Keifer, pp. 43-47.

Fourth Point
That you begin preparing major feasts and seasons.
 a. The Church year began with SUNDAY first...then Easter, the three days, The lenten season, The christmas/epiphany season, the advent season. Ideally, this is how the year should be planned.
 b. In modern times, the School year of September beginnings, May endings, and summer vacation dominate even the four seasons.
 c. Examine your parish celebrations (anniversaries, Bishop arrivals, etc.)
 d. Re-read, Huck pp. 49-54.

Fifth Point
That the presider/celebrant must be present.
 a. Open a discussion about the importance of the presider and the effect he has on the total celebration. Discuss style, not personality.
 b. Re-read Donner, Mongoven, pp. 55-57.
  Read Hovda, *Strong, Loving and Wise*, The Liturgical Press

Summary
Summarize the learning in today's session
Preparation, Assembly, Feasts, Presider.

Suggested Activity: Review what has been said about <u>your</u> parish's assembly, feasts and presider.

NEXT CLASS:
 Topic: "The Place of Music in the Celebration"
 Assignment: *Read Music In Catholic Worship* #23-41

SESSION THREE

The Place of Music in the Celebration

Music in Catholic Worship # 23-66.
Music in Catholic Worship: NPM Commentary, pp. 67-81

TEACHER'S PREPARATION:
Read first the document sections, then the lesson plan outline below, then the pertinent sections connected with each point. Make notes from the three articles as you go.

GOAL:
For the class to examine the three major judgments
* The Liturgical Judgement
* The Musical Judgement
* The Pastoral Judgement
* And to apply these judgments to a specific liturgy within the parish.

CLASS OUTLINE:
First Point:
Review that the focus of today's session is on the role of music in the liturgy. You might want to begin the session with a brief discussion of the role of music in our society, and the role of music in worship. You might want to find out what type of secular music people like. You might want to distinguish between music to be listened to, to be danced to, to be sung. Who performs which music?
How do you go about judging music used in the liturgy? Can anything be used at any time?

Second Point:
The Liturgical Judgement
 a. Music for the liturgy performs a function related to structure of the liturgy. There are three elements: the structure of the liturgy, the text, and who performs it.
 b. Re-read Cunningham, pp. 73-77.

Third Point:
The Musical Judgement
   a. A competent musician must make this decision. A trained musician may not always be competent. An untrained musician is almost always not competent. But the musical judgement is not the only judgement to make about music.
   b. Re-read Gutfreund, pp. 67-71.

Fourth Point:
The Pastoral Judgement
   a. The Pastoral judgement takes into account that the assembly gathered for liturgy is a dynamic, changing group of believers. It is not an excuse for mediocre, banal, or bad music. But it does recognize that some things in parishes take time or happen gradually.
   b. "No set of rubrics or regulations of itself will ever achieve a truly pastoral celebration of the sacramental rites."
   c. Re-read Funk, pp. 79-81.

Fifth Point:
Apply these three judgments to a Sunday celebration within your parish community.
   a. Discuss who is competent to make musical judgments. Discuss the structure, the text, and the roles. What is the role of the choir, cantor, organist. Does the congregation know that it has a musical role?

Summary

Suggested Activity: Review the three judgments and determine which is in need of the most work in your parish.

NEXT CLASS:
   Topic: "A General Consideration of the Introductory Rites and the Liturgy of the Word" And "The Application of the Principles of Celebration of Music in Eucharistic Liturgy".
   Assignment: Read, *Music In Catholic Worship* # 42-49; # 50-78

SESSION FOUR

The Role of Music in Entrance Rite and The Liturgy of the Word

Music in Catholic Worship,
 The Entrance Rite *#42-45, and 61, 65-66*
 The Liturgy of the Word *#45-46, 55, 63, 69, 71, 74.*
Music in Catholic Worship: NPM Commentary, pp. 97-116

GOALS:
* To provide a basic overview of the structure of the Mass
* To show the role of music in the introductory rites
* To show the role of music in the Liturgy of the Word
* To evaluate the situation in your parish

CLASS OUTLINE
First Point:
 The Basic Overview of the Structure of the Mass.
 a. The divisions of the Mass, Entrance, Liturgy of the Word, Liturgy of the Eucharist, and Dismissal are well known by now. Within each division, different parts or rites of the Mass have developed. Some are optional, some vary, some remain the same. (*Music in Catholic Worship* #44-49)
 b. The parts of the mass have a function to perform. This function is performed by a rite (action and words). The rite is well performed if it achieves its specific function. Thus each person should know the function of the rite(s).
 c. Re-read Kavanagh, pp. 97-103.

Second Point:
 The Role of Music in the Introductory Rites.
 a. The purpose of the Introductory Rites "help the assembly become a worshipping community and to

prepare them for listening to God's Word and celebrating the Eucharist.

    b. The elements that are given to us for this purpose are Procession accompanied by a song, concluded with a prayer. Additional elements of Greeting, Penitential Rite, Glory to God, and optional rites of Sprinkling must be used with discretion so as not to clutter the purpose of the procession.

    c. Name the challenges connected with preparing an effective entrance rite: e.g., starting on time, music rehearsal and liturgical formation of the community, a procession that works in gathering the people, music appropraite to procession, not too much music, etc.

    Re-read Keifer, pp. 105-108.

Third Point:
The Role of Music in the Liturgy of the Word.

    a. Review the structure and function of the Liturgy of the Word. The primary purpose is to enter into a dialogue between God and the Assembly.

    b. The Assembly accepts the word proclaimed through sung response, silent response, homily, creed, and prayer of the faithful. Explain the function of each of these parts of the Mass.

    c. Explain the different functions of the music: responsorial Psalm as a response between sections of the assembly, prayer of the faithful as litany to be sung in a repetitive manner.

    d. Re-read Collins, pp. 111-117.

Fourth Point:
To evaluate the situation in our parish.

    a. Discuss: What is the awareness or feeling in our community at the end of the introductory rites?

    b. Discuss: In the liturgy of the word, there is a dialogue between the ministers proclaiming the word and the assembly responding to the word. How clear is the dialogue in our parish?
Are the readers and homilists listened to?

    c. With what care are the elements prepared and presented? The procession, the prayer, the readings, the homily, the responsive music, the prayers for others?

d. The purpose of this discussion is not to have general discussion, but to name as accurately as possible the areas of concern in the celebration of the introductory rites and liturgy of the word. In short, using the principles contained in *Music in Catholic Worship*, name the problems that exist in your parish.

NEXT CLASS
   Topic: "The Liturgy of the Eucharist"
   (A General Consideration of the Structure of the Mass and the Application of the Principles of Celebration of Music in Eucharistic Liturgy)
   Assignment: Re-read *Music in Catholic Worship* # 42-78, pay special attention to The Eucharistic Prayer #47, 56-58, and the Communion Rite # 48, 59, 62, 67-68, 72.

SESSION FIVE
The Liturgy of the Eucharist

Music in Catholic Worship
  Eucharistic Prayer #47, 56-58,
  The Communion Rite #48, 59, 62, 67-68, 72.
Music in Catholic Worship: NPM Commentary, pp. 119-131.

GOALS:
* To deepen the appreciation for the liturgy of the eucharist
* To examine closely the eucharistic prayer
* To indicate the elements and their function of the communion rite
* The dismissal as a sending
* To review how the liturgy of the word and liturgy of the eucharistic are related

CLASS OUTLINE:
First Point:
To deepen the appreciation for the liturgy of the eucharist.
   a. The structure of the eucharistic liturgy is preparation for eucharist, eucharistic prayer of blessing, preparation for communion, and communion rite. The dismissal rite concludes the eucharistic celebration.

   b. The theology of the Eucharist should stress the centrality of God the Father, the action of worship by the assembly, and clarify that Jesus is present to perform the act of worship in the name of the assembly. The elements of covenant renewal, blessing, and offering should be clarified.

Second Point:
To examine closely the Eucharistic Prayer.
   a. The eucharistic prayer of blessing is the central act of the liturgy. The preparation rite (Collection and presentation of gifts, prayers of blessing, prayer over the gifts) should not dominate the eucharistic prayer.
   b. The dramatic movement of the eucharistic prayer from preface, to institutional narrative, to

climatic offering and doxology should be stressed.

    c. The three Acclamations are explained: The HOLY as an act of joining with the eternal Song of Praise in the Heavenly Worship, the MEMORIAL ACCLAMATION as following the mandate to "Make Memory of HIM" and the AMEN as a covenant ratification of the entire assembly. Re-read Ryan, pp. 119-13.

Third Point:
    To indicate the elements of the Communion Rite and their function.
    a. Communion has a twofold meaning: A union or bonding with Christ and with the assembled members.
    b. The specific elements of the Rite and their functions are:

The Our Father, with prayer and conclusion - to call God "Father" is an act of worship, expressing the bond of parent-child relationship with God, the source of our life, as well as the bond of brother and sister with all who pray the prayer.

The Peace Greeting - is what Christ left us during his resurrection appearances. Peace with one another is a sign of Christ's presence among us.

The communion procession, followed by thanksgiving prayer - the ritual action is a procession and sharing of bread and wine, with the two-fold meaning of joining with one another to eat the ritual meal. It is union with Christ and with one another.

Re-read McManus, pp. 125-131.

Fourth Point:
    The Dismissal: *The role of the dismissal is to send the assembly on a mission. Music in Catholic Worship #49*

Fifth Point:
    To review how the liturgy of the word and liturgy of the eucharist are related.

a. The acts of gathering, listening and responding are central to the Mass. Learning the human skills of hospitality, attentive listening, and giving ourselves are the activities of the assembly at the liturgy.

b. The rites (words and gestures) are to assist our activities. How are we doing at our parish?

NEXT CLASS:

Topic: "The Sacraments of Baptism, Anointing of the Sick, Reconciliation, Confirmation and Marriage, and Burial Rites"

Assignment: Read Music in *Catholic Worship* # 79-83, and 84

SESSION SIX

The Sacraments of Baptism, Anointing of the Sick, Reconciliation, Confirmation and Marriage, and the Burial Rites

Music in Catholic Worship # 79-83, and 84.
Music in Catholic Worship: NPM Commentary, pp. 137-171.

GOALS:
  * To stress the importance of the whole sacramental life of the parish as something more
  * To examine, in brief fashion, the sacraments of baptism, anointing of the sick, reconciliation, confirmation and marriage, and the burial rites
  * To conclude the class

CLASS OUTLINE
First Point:
  To stress the importance of more than the Eucharist in the sacramental life of the parish.
  a. In 1972, when *Music in Catholic Worship* was written, the sacraments had not been revised. Therefore, the text of *Music in Catholic Worship* is out of date regarding the sacraments.
  b. The best alternate sources are the introductions to each of the sacraments found before the rite itself. e.g. General Instruction of the Roman Missal is in the Sacramentary. (cf. Ralph Keifer, *To Give Thanks and Praise*) and Instruction for Lectors is in the front of the Lectionary (cf. Ralph Keifer, *To Hear and Proclaim*).
  c. Re-read Ciferni, pp. 137-141.

Second Point:
  To examine, in brief fashion, The sacraments of baptism, anointing of the sick, reconciliation, confirmation and marriage, and the burial rites.
  a. Baptism - the the rite of christian initiation of adults must be studied by liturgy committees. (also re-

read: Lewinski, pp. 143-147.

b. Anointing of the sick - the role of physical healing of all illness rather than preparation for death must be clarified with this sacrament. Re-read Streifel, pp. 149-153.

c. Reconciliation - doing penance and the sacrament of reconciliation need to be related. Re-read Munch, pp. 155-161.

d. Confirmation should be joined to the rites of initiation (baptism, confirmation and eucharist). The practical aspects of how marriages are prepared for and celebrated in our parish especially in terms of music can be discussed. (cf. Covino, *Celebrating Marriage*)

e. While not a sacrament, funerals and burial rites should be discussed, especially in terms of music and community involement.

To Conclude the Class

a. Each teacher will want to sum up according to their own approach and direction.

b. Some elements that you might want to consider in this summary or conclusion:

-a thank you for continued attendance and if members of a parish liturgy team, for their generosity of time and talent.

-the importance of further study.

Some suggestions:

deeper on the liturgical aspects of the Mass (Johnson, *The Mystery of Faith*; Keifer, *To Give Thanks and Praise*)

more on the practical aspects of Liturgy Committees: (Baker and Ferrone, *Liturgy Committee Basics*)

more on the Ministers of the Liturgy (Johnson, *Minsters of Music*)

Bibliography

Bishop's Comittee on the Liturgy, *Music in Catholic Worship,* 1982 ed, Publications Department, USCC, Washington, DC.

Funk, Virgil C., *Music in Catholic Worship: NPM Commentary,* The Pastoral Press, $5.95.

Keifer, Ralph, *To Give Thanks and Praise, General Instruction of the Roman Missal with Commenatry for Musicians and Priests,* The Pastoral Press, $4.95

Keifer, Ralph, *To Hear and Proclaim: Introduction to the Lectionary for Mass with commentary for musicians and priests,* The Pastoral Press, $4.95

Fleming, Austin, *Preparing for Liturgy, A Theology and Spirituality,* The Pastoral Press, $6.95.

Hovda, Robert, *Strong, Loving and Wise,* The Liturgical Press.

Additional Resources For Liturgy Committees

Baker, Thomas and Ferrone, Frank, *Liturgy Committee Basics,* The Pastoral Press, $6.95

Ostdiek, Gilbert, *Catechesis for Liturgy: A program for parish involvement,* The Pastoral Press, $9.95.

Gelineau, Joseph, *Learning to Celebrate, The Mass and Its Music,* The Pastoral Press, $6.95

Johnson, Lawrence J., *The Mystery of Faith: The Minsters of Music,* The Pastoral Press, $5.95

Covino, Paul, *Celebrating Marriage: Preparing the Wedding Liturgy, A Workbook for the Engaged Couple,* The Pastoral Press, $4.95